Beware! See the **EMPEROR SCORPION** raise its stinger!

Make the world's **LARGEST CENTIPEDE** scuttle around your room!

In dual user mode, you and your friend can battle **HERCULES BEETLES.**

Explore the app to uncover incredible facts and stats about the bugs!

CALGARY PUBLIC LIBRARY
AUGUST 2018

D0620911

THIS IS A CARLTON BOOK
Text, design and illustration © Carlton Books Limited 2017

Published in 2017 by Carlton Books Limited
An imprint of the Carlton Publishing Group
20 Mortimer Street, London W1T 3JW

All rights reserved. This book is sold subject to the condition that it may not be reproduced, stored in a retrieval system or transmitted in any form or by any means, electronic, mechanical, photocopying, recording or otherwise, without the publisher's prior consent.

A catalogue record for this book is available from the British Library.

ISBN: 978-1-78312-253-0
Printed in Dongguan, China

Executive editor: Selina Wood
Art editor: Dani Lurie
Design: rockjawcreative.com
Cover design: rockjawcreative.com
Illustrator: Peter Liddiard
Picture research: Steve Behan
Production: Yael Steinitz

Picture credits

The publishers would like to thank the following sources for their kind permission to reproduce the pictures in this book.

2-3. Shutterstock.com, iStockphoto.com (scorpion), Getty Images/Joel Sartore, National Geographic Photo Ark (centipede); 4-5. Diyana Dimitrova/Shutterstock.com; 6. Getty Images/Joel Sartore; 7. (top) Getty Images/Piotr Naskrecki/Minden Pictures, (bottom) Nicolas Reusens/Science Photo Library; 8-9. Nicolas Reusens/Science Photo Library, 9. (top) Cosmin Manci/Shutterstock.com; 10-11. Deepu SG/Alamy Stock Photo; 11. (left) © Biosphoto/Francois Gilson, (right) NHPA/Photoshot; 12-13. Vladimir Wrangel/ Shutterstock.com; 13 (top) Skydie/Shutterstock.com, (bottom) Aleksey Stemmer/ Shutterstock.com; 14. Getty Images/Robin Bush; 15. Mark Moffett/Minden Pictures/ FLPA; 16. (bottom) Getty Images/Alastair Macewen, (centre) Nature Picture Library/ Nature Production; 16-17. Getty Images/Alastair Macewen; 18. Eric Isselee; 18-19. Luc Viatour/www.Lucnix.be; 19. (top) imageBROKER/Alamy Stock Photo; 20. JMK; 20-21. Redmond O. Durrell/Alamy Stock Photo; 21. Mark Moffett/Minden Pictures; 22. (bottom) Ashley Whitworth/Shutterstock.com (top) EPA/Alamy Stock Photo; 22-23. Getty Images/Matt Cardy; 24. Audrey Snider-Bell/Shutterstock.com; 24-25. B & T Media Group Inc./Shutterstock.com; 25. Simon D. Pollard/Science Photo Library; 26-27. Peter Bay/Shutterstock.com; 27. Getty Images/ZSSD/Minden Pictures; 28. Getty Images/Joel Sartore, National Geographic Photo Ark; 28-29. Fabio Lotti/Shutterstock.com; 29. Getty Images/Frank Greenaway; 30-31. Shutterstock.com & iStockphoto.com

Every effort has been made to acknowledge correctly and contact the source and/ or copyright holder of each picture and Carlton Books Limited apologises for any unintentional errors or omissions that will be corrected in future editions of this book.

iEXPLORE

BUGS

Hannah Wilson

Need some help? Check out our useful website for helpful tips
and problem-solving advice:

www.icarlton.co.uk/help

BRING ON THE BUGS!

Insects first crawled around on Earth 480 million years ago, long before the dinosaurs. Today, they are the most successful animal group of all, with about 5 million species. Weird and wonderful, super-strong with super-senses, tiny and toxic or huge and harmless, let's meet them!

WHAT IS AN INSECT?

An insect has six legs and three body sections: a head; a thorax (to which the legs attach); and an abdomen with parts for digesting food and producing young. Many insects have two pairs of wings.

A cricket completing its final mou...

toughened front wing

six legs

hindwing

abdomen

thorax

head

antenna

A TRUE BUG

We tend to use the word "bug" as a general term to describe insects and other creepy crawlies. This assassin bug (above) is a "true bug"— an insect similar to a beetle but jawless and with a softer body.

TOUGH ON THE OUTSIDE

An insect has an exoskeleton — a skeleton on the outside of its body that protects the soft body parts underneath. The exoskeleton is not bone — it's made of chitin, a strong flexible material a bit like fingernails.

Scorpions and spiders, with eight legs and only two body sections, are not insects. They are arachnids, but they do have exoskeletons. As an insect or arachnid grows, its exoskeleton does not. So the bug must moult — the exoskeleton splits and the critter climbs out with a new exoskeleton already in place.

SENSING AND FEEDING

Insects have two antennae to help them feel, taste or smell their surroundings. If the antennae sense dinner, mouthparts spring into action. Beetles have biting jaws to grab and chew prey, while houseflies use a "sponge" to soak up liquids. Mosquitoes have a needle-like tube to pierce skin and suck up blood.

A tiger beetle's jaws

BUG LIFE-CYCLES

Most insects hatch from eggs. The young of some types of insect are called nymphs and as they grow they gradually start to look more like an adult. In other insects, the change from young to adult insect is dramatic — the adult turns out looking very different from the young bug.

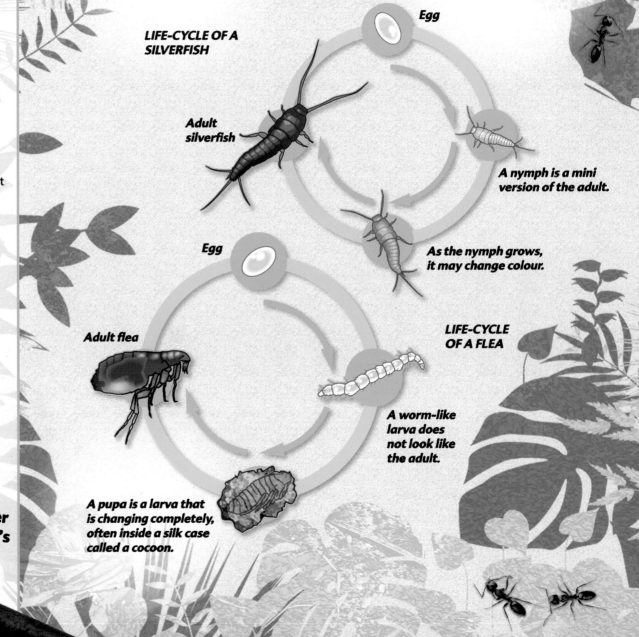

LIFE-CYCLE OF A SILVERFISH

Egg

Adult silverfish

A nymph is a mini version of the adult.

As the nymph grows, it may change colour.

Egg

Adult flea

LIFE-CYCLE OF A FLEA

A worm-like larva does not look like the adult.

A pupa is a larva that is changing completely, often inside a silk case called a cocoon.

HERCULES BEETLE

Meet the mighty Hercules beetle, one of the largest insects on the planet. Its curved claw-like horn alone can reach 10 cm. But it's not all about size — this bug can hiss, stink and even change colour!

NIGHT-TIME NIBBLES

The Hercules beetle is nocturnal. For a midnight feast, it loves nothing better than rotten fruit. Among the leaf litter below rainforest trees, it searches for fallen mangoes and bananas.

.... **thorax horn**

head horn

A BATTLE OF HORNS

Only the male Hercules has horns — the longest extends from its thorax and a second shorter one from its head below. The males lock horns to fight for the chance to mate with a female. One beetle will trap the other between its horns, before lifting it up and slamming it down to claim victory.

GREEN, YELLOW OR BLACK?

The beetle's front wings (the tough protective "wing cases") change colour depending on the rainforest's humidity. When there is lots of moisture in the air, the wings appear black. When there is little moisture, they are olive green or golden yellow.

front wing (wing case)

Bug Data

Latin name: *Dynastes hercules*

SIZE Up to 18 cm long, including horn

WEIGHT Up to 38 g

HABITAT Floor of rainforest

LOCATION Central and South America

DIET Tropical fruits. The young eat decaying plants and wood

LIFESPAN 3 years

iEXPLORE

INTERACTIVE BUG SAFARI

DUAL USER MODE

BATTLING BEETLES!

Grab a friend with a second device, then battle your male Hercules beetles.

TRICKS OF THE TRADE

If a hungry bird or rat appears, the beetle will fly away or burrow down into leaves or soil to hide. If that doesn't work, it can release foul-smelling chemicals or hiss a warning by rubbing its abdomen against its wing cases.

QUEEN ALEXANDRA'S BIRDWING BUTTERFLY

The Queen Alexandra's birdwing is the largest butterfly in the world. The female has brown patterned wings stretching to almost 30 cm. The male (main picture) is smaller but, shimmering bluey green and yellow, is just as impressive.

a female feeding

FLOWERY FOOD

This huge butterfly feeds on flowering rainforest vines. It uncurls its long proboscis, a tube-like mouthpart, and dips it into the vine's flower to sip the sweet nectar. Like bees, butterflies spread pollen among flowers, helping them to fertilize and produce seeds.

antenna for smelling and for sensing vibrations

proboscis

Bug Data

Latin name: *Ornithoptera alexandrae*

SIZE Wingspan up to 27 cm (female) or 20 cm (male)

WEIGHT Up to 12 g

HABITAT Rainforest

LOCATION Papua New Guinea

DIET Nectar from flowering vines. The young eat decaying plant matter

LIFESPAN 4 months as an adult butterfly

LAYING EGGS

The female butterfly tastes a plant to see if it is suitable to lay her eggs on. She taps the plant with her legs to release its juices, then tastes them with special cells on her leg. A butterfly's sense of taste is 200 times stronger than a human's!

TOXIC CATERPILLAR

A butterfly egg hatches into a larva called a caterpillar. The caterpillar of the Queen Alexandra's birdwing eats its own eggshell, then munches on vine leaves, absorbing their poisonous chemicals. The chemicals don't harm the caterpillar, but they do harm hungry predators. The caterpillar's bright red spines act as a warning to birds and small mammals: *don't eat me, I'm toxic!*.

METAMORPHOSIS

When the caterpillar is fully grown, it makes silk to help it hang under a leaf or branch. Then it changes into a pupa, called a chrysalis, and begins to change. After about six weeks, the metamorphosis (transformation from larva to adult) is complete and the butterfly opens its wings for the first time.

front wing

hindwing

iEXPLORE

INTERACTIVE BUG SAFARI

MEET A SUPERSIZED

QUEEN ALEXANDRA'S BIRDWING BUTTERFLY

Make this giant-winged beauty fly around your room!

MADAGASCAR HISSING COCKROACH

Walking through a Madagascan rainforest and hear a hiss? It may not be a snake — it may be 10 cm of giant cockroach! Let's meet this noisy roach and find out why it's one of the toughest bugs on the planet.

thorax

head

SQUEEEEZE!

Unlike most cockroaches, this hissing bug doesn't have wings and it can't fly. But like the others, its body is oval and flattened. So if it needs to make a quick getaway, it can squeeze into a narrow space under a log or stone to hide.

HISSSSSS!

Many insects rub body parts together to make noises, but the male Madagascar hissing cockroach has an unusual technique — it pushes air out of the breathing holes on its abdomen. The hisses attract females or scare away predators.

SURVIVAL EXPERTS

Cockroaches have a reputation for being tough. They can survive weeks without food and cope with extreme temperatures that would kill most animals. They can even survive decapitation! Yes, a cockroach can live for several weeks without its head! Clotting prevents blood loss and — don't forget — the roach breathes through holes in its abdomen.

DARK OR LIGHT?

This big bug is nocturnal — it likes to hide in darkness. However, many nocturnal insects, such as moths, are attracted to light — possibly because they use light (normally moonlight) to navigate or because they are trying to escape from dark foliage into bright moonlit sky.

Bug Data

Latin name: *Gromphadorhina portentosa*

SIZE	Up to 10 cm
WEIGHT	Up to 23 g
HABITAT	Floor of rainforest
LOCATION	Madagascar, Africa
DIET	Decaying fruit and plant material; smaller insects
LIFESPAN	About 3.5 years

leg with pads and hooks to aid climbing

males have large humps for combat

leathery abdomen

iEXPLORE

INTERACTIVE BUG SAFARI

MEET A SUPERSIZED

MADAGASCAR HISSING COCKROACH

Bring this mighty Madagascan critter to life!

GIANT WETAPUNGA CRICKET

Say "hello" to a wetapunga, one of the chunkiest, heaviest insects of all. This solitary cricket lives a quiet life, hanging out in trees and munching leaves. Just don't try to eat it — it has a fearsome kick!

BIG AND BULKY

Unlike many crickets and grasshoppers, the wetapunga is wingless. It would probably be too heavy to fly anyway — it can barely jump! The heaviest specimen ever recorded weighed 71 g — as much as three mice!

TRICKY KICKS

The wetapunga's huge size, tough exoskeleton and spiky legs are usually enough to stop this big bug becoming anyone's dinner. But if it does need a defensive trick, it can kick up those spiky back legs. The legs make a scary rasping sound as they rub against its abdomen!

ear below knee

long antenna

tough exoskeleton

spiky leg

LAYING EGGS

A female wetapunga uses a large spike on its rear to lay eggs. She uses this "ovipositor" to make a hole in soil or rotten wood. Then she lays several oval eggs, each almost a centimetre long.

iEXPLORE

INTERACTIVE BUG SAFARI

MEET A SUPERSIZED

GIANT WETAPUNGA CRICKET

Make this giant cricket crawl onto your friend's hand!

Bug Data

Little Barrier Island Giant Weta
Latin name: *Deinacrida heteracantha*

SIZE Body length up to 10 cm; legspan up to 20 cm

WEIGHT Average 35 g

HABITAT Forest

LOCATION New Zealand island

DIET Leaves (in the wild)

LIFESPAN About 2 years

UNDER THREAT

Wetapunga are rare, living on just a few islands in New Zealand. Like many endangered animals, human development has destroyed some of their habitat. But predators have been the main problem. Today, rats and feral cats that ate these bugs have been eradicated and the wetapunga population is protected.

JAPANESE GIANT HORNET

The Japanese giant hornet has venom powerful enough to kill a human, so beware, especially if you're a honeybee! Five times bigger than a bee and 20 times heavier, when this killer wasp attacks a bee, it never gives up. Ever.

THE QUEEN AND HER NEST

In the spring, a queen Japanese giant hornet burrows into rotten tree roots. She chews up wood and shapes it into hexagonal papery cells. In each cell, she lays a single egg. Eventually, the nest (right) may be home to 700 worker wasps, which are mostly female. All the hornets have black and yellow warning stripes, but only females have stingers.

BEEHIVE BATTLE

If a hornet scout finds a beehive, it marks it with a chemical scent then returns to its nest to get reinforcements. A swarm of hornets then attack the hive, biting off the bees' heads with powerful mandibles (jaws). They don't stop until all the bees are dead. Just 30 hornets can kill 30,000 bees in a few hours.

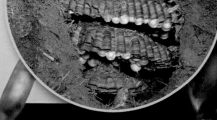

warning stripes on abdomen

mandible

compound eye (hundreds of separate eye units)

antenna

BALL OF BEES

Some bees fight back. Japanese honeybees quickly detect the chemical left by the hornet scout. Five hundred of them will swarm around the hornet, trapping it inside a ball of bees. They vibrate their wing muscles to heat the hornet, killing it before it can fly off to report the beehive's location.

HUNGRY HORNETS

If the hornets do conquer a beehive, they chew up the bees' larvae, return to their nest and vomit up the food for their own young. The adults can't eat solid food themselves. They feed on honey from the beehive, tree sap and a liquid produced by their own larvae.

Bug Data

Latin name: *Vespa mandarinia*

SIZE Almost 8 cm (queen's wingspan); about 5 cm (queen's body length)

WEIGHT 1.6 g (worker); about 3 g (queen)

HABITAT Forest, mountains, farmland

LOCATION Japan, China and other parts of eastern Asia

DIET Adults eat honey, tree sap and fruit liquids. Larvae eat insects vomited up by adults

LIFESPAN 1 year (queen)

iEXPLORE

INTERACTIVE BUG SAFARI

MEET A SUPERSIZED

JAPANESE GIANT HORNET

Beware! There's a killer wasp flying around your room.

GIANT SHIELD MANTIDS

With their alien appearance, peculiar upright posture and claws longer than those of all other insects, it's no wonder ancient civilizations thought these giant mantids had magical powers. And they're certainly powerful — those claws can ensnare a mouse, lizard or frog!

AMBUSH PREDATOR

The mantid is a patient hunter. Camouflaged among the leaves, it will lie in wait for a tasty insect, mouse or frog to walk by. Then, with lightning speed, the mantid pounces, reaching forward to grab its victim with its spiky front legs. Dinner-time!

SUPER SIGHT

Forward-facing eyes sit either side of the mantid's triangular head, giving the bug binocular vision. This means that its eyes work together, helping the bug to calculate distances accurately when hunting. Mantids are the only insects able to turn their heads around to look behind them.

large forward-facing eyes

long thin thorax

spiky front leg

MASTER OF DISGUISE

Green or brown like a plant and with long thin legs like twigs, mantids are masters of disguise. Some types sway to mimic branches blowing in the breeze, while others have thoraxes or wings shaped like leaves or petals. A few mantids can even turn black after a forest fire to match the burnt landscape!

FEARSOME FEMALE

If threatened, both male and female mantids put on an aggressive performance, raising their front legs high and fanning out wings to appear as large as possible. But only the female indulges in cannibalism — after mating, she often bites off a male's head before gobbling him up!

Bug Data

Main photo: *Giant Malaysian Shield mantid*
Latin name: *Rhombodera basalis*

SIZE Up to 15 cm

HABITAT Forest, rainforest, grassland

LOCATION East Asia

DIET Mainly insects and spiders; sometimes lizards, frogs, mice

LIFESPAN Up to 1 year

wing

abdomen

iEXPLORE

INTERACTIVE BUG SAFARI

MEET A SUPERSIZED
GIANT SHIELD MANTID

Make this creepy critter crawl along your table and more!

DRIVER ANTS

Driver ants may be small, but they are killer critters with powerful jaws. So when a colony of 20 million come marching by, you might just want to step aside!

large armoured head

jaw-like mandible

TYPES OF DRIVER ANT

There are three types of driver ant in a colony; workers, which are female and wingless (main picture); males, who have long bodies and wings, and are nicknamed "sausage flies" (left); and finally, there is just one queen. The queen is the largest ant in the world — 5 cm long. She can lay up to 100,000 eggs in one day!

SENSING SCENTS

Incredibly, the worker ants are completely blind. They communicate by releasing chemical scents. The ants' antennae have millions of hairs and tiny "pits" (sensitive hollows or patches) that detect these scents and pick up vibrations.

FEEDING FRENZY

An insect caught in a swarm of driver ants has little chance of escape. The soldiers manoeuvre their razor-sharp jaws to dismember the prey quickly. Driver ants can even conquer a sleeping cow, filling its nostrils and mouth, suffocating it. The smaller worker ants carry chunks of the meat back to the nest.

INTERACTIVE BUG SAFARI

iEXPLORE

MEET A SUPERSIZED

DRIVER ANT

Watch out for the jaws on these incredible marching ants!

MASSIVE MARCHING ARMY

When millions of driver ants are on the move, they are unstoppable. Scouring the leaf litter for food, the smaller workers march in a column guarded on either side by larger workers, called soldiers. Ditches or streams pose no problem — the ants build bridges with their bodies!

Bug Data

Driver ant group (Latin name): *Dorylus* sp.

SIZE Queen, 5 cm; soldier, 1 cm; male "sausage fly", up to 2.5 cm

HABITAT Forest, grasslands

LOCATION Africa

DIET Insects, sleeping cattle

LIFESPAN Up to 1 year (workers); several years (queen)

LORD HOWE ISLAND STICK INSECT

Often reddish dark brown and always big and chunky, the Lord Howe Island stick insect is nicknamed the "land lobster"! But you'd be lucky to meet one — this is probably the rarest insect in the world.

dark or reddish brown colour

WHAT IS A STICK INSECT?

Not all stick insects are thick and chunky. Many have long slender bodies and legs that resemble... sticks! This camouflage helps them avoid attack, and some can also fly away from danger. The Lord Howe Island bug is wingless — but it's good at running back to its daytime hiding place in soil or leaf litter.

antenna for sensing

BACK FROM THE DEAD

This big bug was thought to be extinct, but in 2001, two scientists wanted to make sure. One night, they climbed a steep rocky outcrop (left) that rose from the sea off the coast of Australia, searching for this nocturnal insect. Beneath a bush on a cliff, they found 24 of the stick insects, thought to be the world's entire population. Today, the bugs have been bred in zoos and returned to their rocky island home.

SNUGGLING UP

Very unusually for insects, male and female Lord Howe Island stick insects form close bonds. At night, they snuggle up together in pairs, the male wrapping three legs protectively around the female.

Bug Data

Latin name: *Dryococelus australis*

SIZE Up to 15 cm
WEIGHT Up to 25 g
HABITAT Among vegetation
LOCATION Rocky ocean outcrop near Lord Howe Island, off east coast of Australia
DIET Plants
LIFESPAN 12 to 18 months

strong, armoured leg

GOING SOLO

Despite her close relationship with the male, the female stick insect sometimes produces babies without him. It is this ability that may have helped the tiny island population survive. In one lifetime, the female lays about 300 eggs, usually in soil. The nymphs that hatch are bright green in colour.

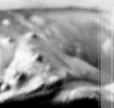

iEXPLORE

INTERACTIVE BUG SAFARI

MEET A SUPERSIZED

LORD HOWE ISLAND STICK INSECT

Make this stick-legged survivor scuttle around.

GOLIATH BIRD-EATING SPIDER

It's night in the jungle and the Goliath bird-eating tarantula creeps out of its underground burrow in search of dinner. A massive 170 g, no spider is heavier. It's not just birds that better watch out, this giant may sink its fangs into insects, mice, frogs or lizards.

SAC OF SILK

The female lays up to 150 eggs in the burrow, spinning a sac of silk to protect them. She also adds a layer of her itchy bristles to stop bugs devouring the eggs. Once hatched, the spiderlings live inside the burrow for a few years, moulting several times as they grow, until they are large enough to head outside.

eight eyes

jaws

ARACHNID ANATOMY

Spiders are arachnids, not insects. They have two body segments (an abdomen and a cephalothorax, which is a combined thorax and head). They have eight legs and two pedipalps, which — for spiders — resemble short legs and are used for sensing.

DINNER-TIME

This giant spider has giant 2.5-cm-long fangs. It uses them to bite and crush its prey. Then the tarantula releases digestive juices and the victim is dissolved into a mush, which the spider slurps up with its short straw-like mouth.

HAIRY SCARY

Despite their eight eyes, tarantulas have poor vision. Instead, they feel their way about using the sensitive hairs on their legs. The hair on a Goliath birdeater's abdomen (left) has another purpose — it's a weapon. The spider rubs its abdomen with its back legs to release the harmful bristles, which cause severe itching and can kill a small creature.

bristly leg

pedipalp

iEXPLORE

INTERACTIVE BUG SAFARI

MEET A SUPERSIZED

GOLIATH BIRD-EATING SPIDER!

Release a big, hairy tarantula spider!

Bug Data

Latin name: *Theraphosa blondi*

SIZE Legspan up to 28 cm; body length up to 12 cm

WEIGHT Up to 170 g

HABITAT Floor of rainforest

LOCATION South America

DIET Mainly worms and insects, but also frogs, lizards, snakes, mice, occasionally birds

LIFESPAN Up to 25 years (female). Up to 6 years for a male

EMPEROR SCORPION

Check out this eight-legged, armoured arachnid. As long as your forearm, the emperor scorpion is black and glossy with huge claws. And watch out — there's a sting in its tail!

STABBING STINGER

The sharp curved stinger may look nasty, but its venom, like the venom of many large scorpions, is mild. Only young scorpions use their stinger to kill prey. An adult uses it for defence. The scorpion will raise its tail and stab the stinger at a hungry bat, bird or lizard.

POWERFUL PINCERS

This big bad beast's real power lies in its claws, which are adapted pedipalps. Covered in sensitive hairs, they help the bug detect the movements of small creatures. The scorpion chases its prey, grabbing it with the pincers and crushing it before eating.

stinger

abdomen

claw-like pedipalp

cephalothorax

UNDERGROUND HOMES

Termites are a favourite snack for emperor scorpions, so they will often dig burrows in termite mounds to set up home. Burrows under logs or leaf litter also keep the scorpions safe from predators. Emperor scorpions are sociable critters, living in groups of up to 15.

iEXPLORE

INTERACTIVE BUG SAFARI

MEET A SUPERSIZED

EMPEROR SCORPION

Watch out! This scary scorpion may raise its stinger if its disturbed!

BABIES ON BOARD

About 15 baby scorpions, like tiny miniature adults, can hitch a ride on their mother's back. She will provide food and protection until they are mature enough to fend for themselves. The babies are white at first — they grow darker with each moult.

Bug Data

Latin name: *Pandinus imperator*

SIZE Average 20 cm

WEIGHT Up to 30 g

HABITAT Rainforest, grassland

LOCATION West Africa

DIET Termites and other insects; sometimes spiders, mice, lizards

LIFESPAN 5 years

AMAZONIAN GIANT CENTIPEDE

Here comes the largest centipede in the world. Thirty centimetres long with venomous claws and a bad temper, this is one lean mean fighting-machine.

flat head shaped like a shield

LOTS OF LEGS

Centipedes have more than six legs so they are not insects. Like millipedes, they are actually myriapods, meaning "10,000 feet". The Amazonian giant centipede doesn't have quite that many — it has up to 46 legs with a separate pair on each body segment. The rear legs are longer than the others, and spiny — perfect for scaring away hungry predators.

CLAWS THAT KILL

The front legs of the centipede have adapted to become claws — venomous claws. Using them to seize a mouse or lizard, the centipede delivers a sharp stab to inject the venom, immobilizing the prey and often killing it. Trapped in the centipede's coiled body, the victim is powerless to escape.

body segment

long spiny back leg

venomous claw

BATS, BEWARE!

A cave is the perfect hunting ground for a giant centipede — it's dark, damp and full of flying food. Hanging from the cave roof by its rear legs, the giant centipede waits. Suddenly, a bat flies past and the centipede strikes, grabbing the prey with its fearsome claws.

DARK DAMP HOME

Unlike insects, a centipede's exoskeleton does not have a waxy waterproof covering to keep in moisture. To stop its body drying out, it must live in dark damp places, under rocks and logs or in soil or leaf litter. Being nocturnal also helps — the centipede comes out to hunt in the cool of the night.

antenna

iEXPLORE

INTERACTIVE BUG SAFARI

MEET A SUPERSIZED

AMAZONIAN GIANT CENTIPEDE

Beware! See this creepy critter come to life!

Bug Data

Latin name: *Scolopendra gigantea*

SIZE Up to 30 cm

HABITAT Warm, damp tropical-forest floors, under rocks, leaves or in soil

LOCATION Amazon rainforest and other parts of northern South America

DIET Insects, worms, snails, lizards, toads, mice, birds, bats

LIFESPAN 10 years

RECORD-BREAKING BUGS

Beetles are the **MOST COMMON** type of insect with about 400,000 known species. But if we could count individual insects, ants are the most common. There are about 100 trillion of the crawling critters!

The fire beetle, with its two green glowing spots, is the **MOST LUMINOUS** insect of all.

Monarch butterflies undertake what may be the **LONGEST INSECT MIGRATION**, travelling about 8,000 km from Canada to Mexico.

The **LONGEST** insect in the world is a Chinese stick insect, measuring more than 60 cm!

A tiny froghopper bug recorded the **HIGHEST JUMP** ever. It leapt up 70 cm — about the same as a person jumping twice the height of the Statue of Liberty!

The female mayfly is one of the **SHORTEST-LIVING** insects. As an adult, she may live for only five minutes!

A queen termite may be the **LONGEST-LIVING** insect. She can live for 50 years!

The **LARGEST INSECT OF ALL TIME** is a prehistoric dragonfly with a 70-cm wingspan!

The **MOST DANGEROUS** insect to humans is the mosquito. More than 200 million people catch malaria from mosquito bites each year, resulting in hundreds of thousands of deaths.